T0166699

The Little Book of Dinosaurs

Cherie Winner

MINNETONKA, MINNESOTA

The author thanks Dr. John Foster, Curator of Paleontology at the Museum of Western Colorado, and George Callison, Ph.D., for so graciously sharing their knowledge of dinosaurs.

Designed by Joe Fahey
Edited by Jill Anderson

Two-Can Publishing
11571 K-Tel Drive
Minnetonka, MN 55343
www.two-canpublishing.com

Library of Congress Cataloging-in-Publication Data

Winner, Cherie.
   The little book of dinosaurs / by Cherie Winner.
     p. cm.
   Includes index.
   Summary: "Explains what makes a dinosaur a dinosaur and introduces a number of dinosaur species, which are organized by common physical characteristics"—Provided by publisher.
   ISBN 1-58728-484-7 — ISBN 1-58728-516-9 (pbk.)
   1. Dinosaurs—Juvenile literature. I. Title.
   QE861.5.W66 2005
   567.9–dc22

                                        2004028030

1 2 3 4 5 6 10 09 08 07 06 05

Printed in Thailand

Contents

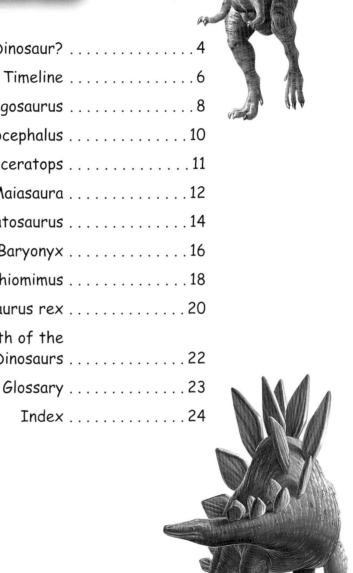

What Is a Dinosaur?

Dinosaurs were **reptiles** that roamed the Earth millions of years ago. Like other reptiles, dinosaurs were covered with tough pieces of skin called scales. Their babies hatched from eggs.

What made dinosaurs different from other reptiles was their hind legs. They had special hips and ankles that helped them grow bigger, stand taller, and run faster than other reptiles.

Many other kinds of reptiles lived at the same time as dinosaurs. Some of them cruised the seas or soared overhead. Those were not dinosaurs. Dinosaurs kept at least two feet on the ground.

4

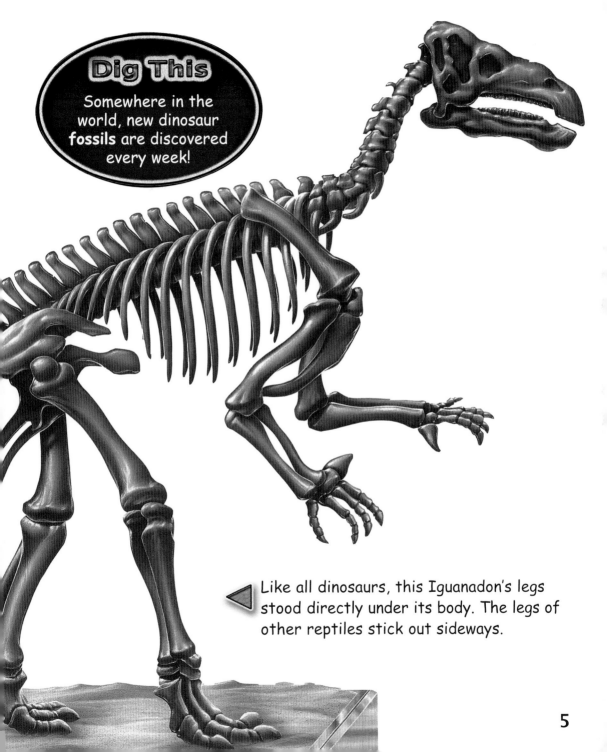

Dig This

Somewhere in the world, new dinosaur **fossils** are discovered every week!

Like all dinosaurs, this Iguanadon's legs stood directly under its body. The legs of other reptiles stick out sideways.

5

Dinosaur Timeline

Dinosaurs lived from 230 to 65 million years ago. But not all dinosaurs lived at the same time. The first dinosaurs were only 3 to 6 feet (1 to 2 m) long, and they stood on two legs. Some were **carnivores,** or meat eaters, that ate lizards, insects, and small mammals. Others were **herbivores,** or plant eaters.

Time ➡

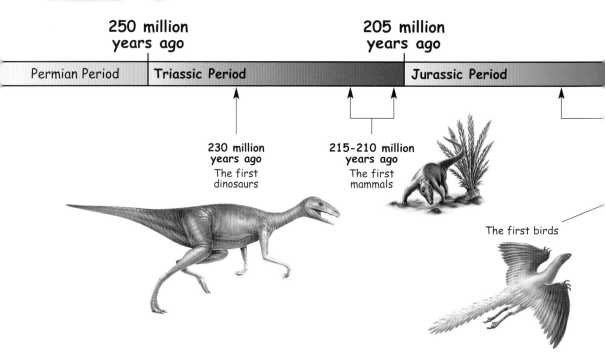

250 million years ago

205 million years ago

| Permian Period | Triassic Period | | Jurassic Period |

230 million years ago
The first dinosaurs

215-210 million years ago
The first mammals

The first birds

Over time, dinosaurs got bigger and took on different shapes. Some began walking on all fours. Their teeth became more specialized for ripping meat or grinding leaves.

Dig This

Stegosaurus became **extinct**, or disappeared from the planet, 70 million years before Tyrannosaurus even showed up!

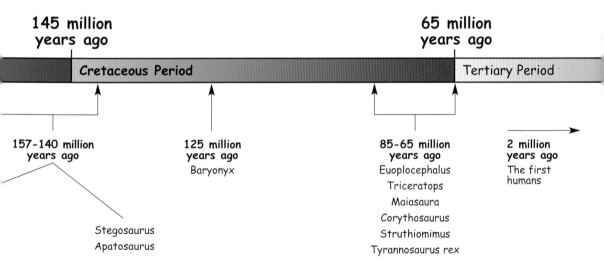

145 million years ago

65 million years ago

Cretaceous Period

Tertiary Period

157-140 million years ago

125 million years ago
Baryonyx

85-65 million years ago
Euoplocephalus
Triceratops
Maiasaura
Corythosaurus
Struthiomimus
Tyrannosaurus rex

2 million years ago
The first humans

Stegosaurus
Apatosaurus

Stegosaurus

(steg-oh-SAWR-us)

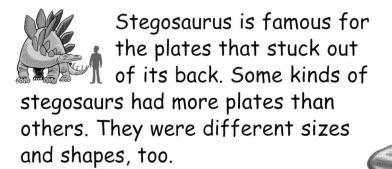

Stegosaurus is famous for the plates that stuck out of its back. Some kinds of stegosaurs had more plates than others. They were different sizes and shapes, too.

A Stegosaurus's plates made it look dangerous. But the plates were not strong enough to protect it from an attacker. Stegosaurus's real weapon was its strong tail. It worked like a whip—but with an extra surprise! Spikes near the end of the tail were nearly 4 feet (1.2 m) long and deadly sharp.

STEGOSAURUS FACTS

When it lived: Late Jurassic,
156 to 140 million years ago

Length: 26 to 30 feet (8 to 9 m)

Height: 9 feet (2.75 m)

Dig This

Despite its prickly
appearance, Stegosaurus
was not a fighter.
It preferred to
munch peacefully
on plants.

Euoplocephalus

(YOU-oh-ploh-SEF-ah-lus)

Euoplocephalus was built more like a tank than a reptile. Bony plates covered most of its body. Sharp horns bristled along its head and back. Only its belly was unprotected. If a **predator** came near, Euoplocephalus could whack the enemy with its club-like tail. If that did not work, the dinosaur dropped to the ground. Few predators were strong enough to flip it over to reach its soft belly.

EUOPLOCEPHALUS FACTS

When it lived: Late Cretaceous, 76 to 65 million years ago

Length: 20 to 23 feet (6 to 7 m)

Height: 6 feet (2 m)

Triceratops

This herbivore wore all of its weapons on its head. A wide, bony frill on the back of its skull covered its neck. Two long horns on its head and a shorter horn on its snout said, "Don't mess with me!"

Unfortunately, predators didn't always get the message. Tyrannosaurus sometimes ate Triceratops for dinner.

TRICERATOPS FACTS

When it lived: Late Cretaceous, 72 to 65 million years ago

Length: 25 feet (8 m)

Height: 15 to 20 feet (4 to 6 m)

Corythosaurus
(co-RITH-oh-SAWR-us)

Maiasaura
(my-oh-SAWR-uh)

Corythosaurus and Maiasaura were part of a group of dinosaurs called hadrosaurs. Hadrosaurs had a flat bill, like a duck. In the back of the mouth, they had hundreds of teeth for shredding leaves.

Hadrosaurs also had a bony crest on the top of the head. Each species' crest was a different shape. Corythosaurus's crest looked like a helmet. These crests may have helped members of a species recognize each other.

Hadrosaurs took good care of their babies. When it was time to raise a family, a mother Maiasaura scooped out a bowl-shaped nest in the dirt. Other mothers made nests nearby. Each mother laid up to 25 eggs. When the babies hatched, they were about 1 foot (30 cm) long. Like all dinosaurs, baby duckbills ate a lot and grew quickly.

CORYTHOSAURUS AND MAIASAURA FACTS

When they lived: Late Cretaceous, 80 to 65 million years ago
Length: 30 feet (9 m)
Height (on four legs): 12 feet (4 m)

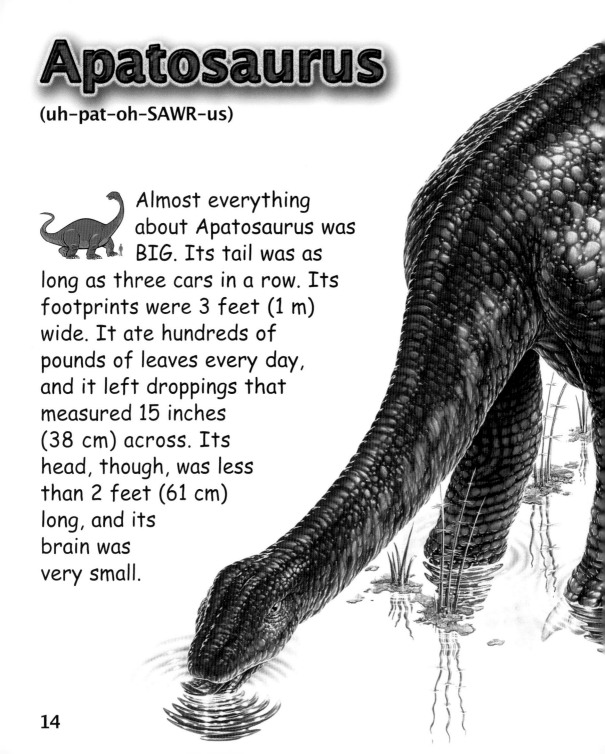

Apatosaurus

(uh-pat-oh-SAWR-us)

Almost everything about Apatosaurus was BIG. Its tail was as long as three cars in a row. Its footprints were 3 feet (1 m) wide. It ate hundreds of pounds of leaves every day, and it left droppings that measured 15 inches (38 cm) across. Its head, though, was less than 2 feet (61 cm) long, and its brain was very small.

Dig This

A female Apatosaurus laid her eggs as she walked along. She did not stay to protect the eggs or raise her babies.

APATOSAURUS FACTS

When it lived: Late Jurassic, 157 to 146 million years ago

Length: 70 feet (21 m)

Height: 22 feet (7 m)

Baryonyx

(bear-ee-ON-icks)

You've probably seen pictures of grizzly bears catching salmon in a river. Now imagine a dinosaur fishing the same way. That's what Baryonyx did. It waded into the water and snagged fish with its 1-foot (30-cm) claws or jagged teeth. So far, Baryonyx is the only dinosaur we know of that ate fish.

Baryonyx also hunted on land. **Paleontologists** have found a Baryonyx fossil that had both fish scales and crushed dinosaur bones in its stomach.

BARYONYX FACTS

When it lived: Early Cretaceous, 125 million years ago

Length: 32 feet (10 m)

Struthiomimus

(strooth-ee-oh-MY-mus)

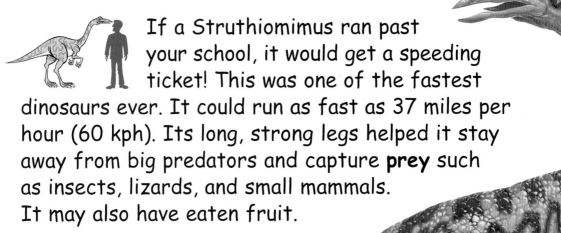

If a Struthiomimus ran past your school, it would get a speeding ticket! This was one of the fastest dinosaurs ever. It could run as fast as 37 miles per hour (60 kph). Its long, strong legs helped it stay away from big predators and capture **prey** such as insects, lizards, and small mammals. It may also have eaten fruit.

STRUTHIOMIMUS FACTS

When it lived: Late Cretaceous, 76 to 70 million years ago

Length: 12 feet (3.7 m)

Height: 6 feet (1.8 m)

Tyrannosaurus rex

(ty-ran-oh-SAWR-us REX)

Tyrannosaurus rex, or T. rex, was one of the biggest predators that ever lived. It hunted alone. We don't know whether it chased its prey or hid and waited for its prey to come by.

Any animal caught by a T. rex was in big trouble. T. rex jaws were 4 feet (1.2 m) long and strong enough to crush bones. Every one of its 60 teeth was as long as your forearm.

TYRANNOSAURUS REX FACTS

When it lived: Late Cretaceous, 85 to 65 million years ago

Length: 40 to 50 feet (12 to 15 m)

Height: 15 to 18 feet (5 to 6 m)

Sometimes Tyrannosaurus's prey got away. One duckbill fossil had marks on its tail bones where a T. rex had bitten it. The duckbill escaped and lived long enough for the bones to heal.

Death of the Dinosaurs

Sixty-five million years ago, something happened that killed almost half of the plant and animal species. Scientists think a huge space rock called a **meteorite** slammed into Earth. Everything nearby was burned up. Dust from the crash made the sky dark for years. With no sunlight, many plants died. So did the animals that ate them.

Some kinds of animals survived, but the dinosaurs died out forever. Lucky for us, their fossils hold amazing secrets.

Glossary

carnivore—an animal that eats mostly meat

Cretaceous Period—the time in Earth's history from 145 to 65 million years ago

extinct—the death of every member of a species of plants or animals

fossil—a rock that contains the remains of an ancient animal or plant

herbivore—an animal that eats mostly leaves, fruits, or other plant material

Jurassic Period—the time in Earth's history from 205 to 145 million years ago

meteorite—a rock from space that lands on the Earth

paleontologist—a scientist who studies ancient animals and plants

predator—an animal that hunts other animals

prey—animals that are hunted by other animals

reptile—a kind of animal with a backbone and scaly skin that lays eggs

Triassic Period—the time in Earth's history from 250 to 205 million years ago

Index